Holy Relationships

CHRISTINE A. ADAMS

MOREHOUSE PUBLISHING

Morehouse Publishing
P.O. Box 1321
Harrisburg, PA 17105

Morehouse Publishing is a division of the Morehouse Group.

Printed in the United States

Jacket design by Trude Brummer

Library of Congress Cataloging-in-Publication Data

Adams, Christine A.
       Holy relationships / Christine A. Adams.
             p.   cm.
       ISBN 0-8192-1738-7
       1. Married people—Prayer-books and devotions—English.
2. Marriage—Religious aspects—Christianity.   3. Intimacy
(Psychology)—Religious aspects—Christianity.   I. Title.
BV4596.M3A27   1998
248.8'44—dc21   97-47708
                                                              CIP

This book is dedicated
to my husband,
Robert J. Butch,
and to the holy relationship
we have found together.

Contents

Purposes of Holy Relationships

Introduction

HOLY RELATIONSHIPS are based on spiritual similarities. Each partner has faced their own personal ordeal and found their way to a more peaceful place. They have done their "soul work" and, through the love of God, found a love of Self. Now, when they reach inside to soul search, they do not see deficiencies but find a completeness, a oneness that comes from God. In other words, they "know" the love of God. There is no gnawing need for a loving connection because the love of God completes them.

Now they can extend their complete self to another, equally as whole. Lovers see no differences in their spiritual selves. There is nothing they would take from the other to complete themselves. They do not come together out of a sense of need, but in a fullness of self.

This book is meant to express the most positive view of a relationship—its holiness. Intentionally, I did not stress aspects of an unholy relationship, but, for clarification, it needs to be stated that all relationships are not holy, and, unless both partners are willing to grow spiritually, the relationship may not function very well.

In an unholy relationship there is a sense of being incomplete and a need to draw from the other. There is an attachment that represents an attempt to reach spiritual unity by merging with another. **It is this sense of personal separation from God that drives lovers to this point of anxiety and insecurity. Both partners see themselves as fragmented from the whole and in need of completeness.**

Examples of unholy relationships are all around us. The other day, on a popular daytime TV show, I saw an example in which a young man had been physically abusive to a young woman. All she asked was that he make a commitment to her and to their unborn child. It seemed clear to everyone in the audience that she should give up this unholy relationship and put her energy into her own life and into the life of the child she carried. She hung on, meekly saying, "But, I love him."

The truth is she does not love herself enough to protect herself, and her child, from him. This situation is not about love, but the lack of it. This girl feels she needs this man "to feel loved." In truth, she does, because she has not discovered her love of Self through the love of God.

When you feel incomplete, you look outside of yourself for security.

One out of two marriages in America ends in divorce. Perhaps the partners have come together for the wrong reasons—sex, money, security, social acceptance. Perhaps they are trying to complete themselves through the other person. Perhaps their relationship operates on material principles rather than spiritual ones. Perhaps they have not discovered that all relationships can have a higher spiritual purpose.

For a relationship to have a higher spiritual purpose, *both* lovers must be "reaching for the spiritual." I stress this point! They may not be at the same place, but spiritual growth must be the priority. If two lovers are not going in the same direction, terrible injustices occur: for example, when one partner extends "trust," which is a spiritual stance, to the other and that partner uses the trust to deceive. This relationship is not operating on a spiritual level because *both* partners aren't involved. This situation could be corrected if the partner who is taking advantage of the other realizes the situation and comes to a more spiritual place.

If your partnership does not "teach love" but is operating out of fear, it is not holy. If you cannot love without conditions, it may be that you have not really defined "love" in a spiritual sense. Both lovers must be honest and extend trust. If the trust is broken, an attempt to mend it can become the spiritual work of the marriage. If the trust is repeatedly broken, you do not have a spiritual bond.

In a way this book is a barometer. It speaks of the guidelines for a very spiritual union. In turn, just by presenting this focus, it may show the deficiencies that exist in an unholy relationship. Upon examination, you may find that your relationship is not premised on spiritual guidelines, or that you don't function spiritually within your marriage, or that your relationship doesn't seem to have a higher purpose. I believe that "God's will for you is Joy" and that God never meant for any person to be abused in a relationship.

When two people come together for spiritual reasons, they are anxious to be guided into new ways to deal with anger, new ways to express feelings, and new ways to emotionally assist their partner when needed. A holy relationship is not based on differences. Each person is complete and whole and is not threatened by the emotions of the other. Each person has needs that are respected and honored in a holy relationship. Abuse occurs when there is a lack of balance—when one person takes from the other. I am writing this book from an ideal position. By using the guidelines in this book in my daily life, by functioning in a spiritual way in my marriage, and by carrying out the spiritual purposes of my marriage, I live in a holy relationship. However, I did not get to this place without having experienced some very unholy relating. For example, I had to know *and walk away from* the darkness of addiction, of infidelity, and of violence to know the light of spirituality, of loyalty, and of peace and love. It was a difficult journey and I was often distraught and confused, but I kept growing spiritually, always developing my relationship with God.

My husband, Bob, made a similar spiritual journey and he rejected the same kinds of spiritual darkness. We met in a higher place and found this holy relationship. However, we could not have come together spiritually if we had not been willing to complete the initial journey. Since we have come together, we continue to grow spiritually—sometimes we move forward together, and sometimes alone. But we always return to each other.

With a new spiritual perspective, there is less fear of loss, less competition, and less tension. We have invited God to share in our marriage. Everyone's relationship history is different. Some may find a holy relationship early in life, some later, and some not at all. Once you find it, you will recognize and appreciate its holiness. Because I have found such rewards in my marriage, I felt compelled to record the guidelines, the functions, and the purposes of a holy relationship. Often, I return to the pages of this book to reflect on the ideas and scriptural references presented here. I hope this book serves you as well as it has me.

What Is a Holy Relationship?

A HOLY RELATIONSHIP is not based on differences. Both partners have looked within themselves and found a spiritual wholeness. By accepting this completion, each lover extends their wholeness to the other, equally as whole. They see no differences between their spiritual selves, for differences are only of the body. Therefore, they do not look to a partner to gain prestige, to possess qualities they lack. Holy partners do not come together to complete themselves or to rob the other. They come together to let the Holy Spirit work through them.

◌

There are different kinds of gifts, but the same Spirit.... All these are the work of one and the same Spirit, and he gives them to each one, just as he determines.

1 CORINTHIANS 12:4, 11 NIV

Guidelines for
Holy Relationships

❧ Guideline 1
God's Will for You Is Joy

WHEN YOU RELATE to your partner in a "holy relationship," the first guideline to keep in mind is "God's will for you is Joy." No matter what happens in your relationship, you are in control of your own happiness. Accept "what is" and you will find joy! No one can find joy while attempting to make someone feel guilty, or blaming someone for their misery. Embrace your own joy and stay connected to God.

I have told you this so that my joy may be in you and that your joy may be complete.

JOHN 15:11 NIV

Find Your Own Joy!

Finding your own joy is your own task. It is not the duty of your lover to always make you happy. Do the inner work necessary to aid your own spiritual growth. Nurture your own soul! Pray and meditate! If you find yourself unhappy, find your way back to joy through your connection with God.

⁓

Pray in the Spirit on all occasions with all kinds of prayers and requests.

EPHESIANS 6:18 NIV

God Gives You Power and Light

God is the source of power and light, and He will send that power and light to you if you ask for help. Ultimately, God's power and light extends through you to those around you. You bring this power and light to your relationship. By staying connected to God, you will be able to let go of life's hardships even when you don't understand them. God is your primary relationship!

I am the vine, you are the branches. He who abides in Me, and I in him, bears much fruit; for without Me you can do nothing.

JOHN 15:5 NKJV

Acceptance Is the Key to Peace

Life may bring loss and sadness to you; however, these things will be easier to bear when you "Let go and let God." By acceptance, you will come to a more peaceful, joyful place. Accepting your lover "where they are at" is essential in a holy relationship. "Where they are at" might not be where you are or where you want them to be, but it is where they are on their journey. This is the reality of your relational situation and your task is to deal with that reality.

~

I have learned the secret of being content in any and every situation.... I can do everything through him who gives me strength.

PHILIPPIANS 4:12, 13 NIV

13

Always Ask: "Is This the Loving Thing to Do?"

No matter what decision you face, ask, "Is this the loving thing to do?" You will be guided to the proper place. Sometimes the most loving thing may be the most difficult to do. Still, that decision may be the one that most enhances your and your lover's spiritual growth.

That God... may fulfill every good purpose of yours and every act prompted by your faith.

2 THESSALONIANS 1:11 NIV

Each Person Must Travel Their Own Spiritual Path

If your partner is having a difficult time spiritually, it is up to him or her to come back to a place of acceptance, resignation, and joy. You may offer loving assistance, but they must do the spiritual work that will return them to God. Just getting out of the way may be the most loving thing you can do.

※

Each one should retain the place in life that the Lord assigned to him and to which God has called him.

1 CORINTHIANS 7:17 NIV

❦ *Guideline 2*
Teach Only Love

*A*NOTHER GUIDELINE for your holy relationship is "Teach only Love." Censure and condemnation have no place in a loving relationship. When love is taught, only love is received as the giving and receiving become one. Loving communication applies to all love situations.

~

Let us love, not in word or speech, but in truth and action.

1 JOHN 3:18 NRSV

Make No Demands!

When you "teach only Love" there are no hidden demands. You might prefer that your partner goes in one particular direction, but do not demand it. Issues that are mutually negotiated are different from unilateral demands. The only person you can make demands on is yourself!

Make every effort to keep the unity of the Spirit through the bond of peace.

EPHESIANS 4:3 NIV

Fear Drives Out Love!

Hidden demands on your partner only mask your own fear. Love and fear cannot live in the same place. A fear of abandonment might cause you to control your lover with fearful demands. Or try to please them to make sure they stay. Make no fearful demands on God, or on others, and you will be happy.

There is no fear in love, but perfect love casts out fear.

1 JOHN 4:18 NRSV

Do Not Be Afraid

Fear itself has no life. It exists only when we give it life. Fear is a parasitic thought that, as we feed and nourish it, appears to take on a life of its own.

⁓

But Jesus came and touched them and said, "Arise, and do not be afraid."

MATTHEW 17:7 NKJV

You Are a Child of God

You are a "child of God," created of Love Itself. By seeing yourself as a child of God, you will come to see that you are never vulnerable. How could you be? You are of God, of Love Itself. Your spirit, soul, inner being, or child is there within you: your divine essence within, unchangeable, immutable.

⌇

Be imitators of God, therefore, as dearly loved children.

EPHESIANS 5:1 NIV

Your Lover Is a Child of God

How do you view your lover and all others you meet? Are they children of God? They are the same as you. When you keep this in mind, you come to understand that you need not like or approve of all of the actions of all people, even of your lover, but you must love the spiritual essence within them.

৴৲

My command is this: Love each other as I have loved you.

JOHN 15:12 NIV

Love without Conditions

ANOTHER GUIDELINE for sacred relationships is "Love without conditions." Really loving someone, without reservations, for who they are is essential to a long-term commitment—to a holy relationship. That means loving someone for their character—their honesty, their loyalty, their perseverance, their kindness, their spirituality, their pride and love of self. It does not mean loving someone for what they could be, or because they say loving things that make you feel good.

My purpose is that they may be encouraged in heart and united in love, so that they may have the full riches of complete understanding.

COLOSSIANS 2:2 NIV

God Loves All of Us

Because we are all God's children, God loves us unconditionally. Within each of us is a place that is of God, of Love Itself. It is our job to love as Christ loved and to encourage others through love. Conditional love is selective in its judgments as to when love can be offered and withheld. We are all asked to love completely, to see others through the accepting eyes of Christ.

༄

Encourage each other to build each other up.
1 THESSALONIANS 5:11 TLB

❦ *Guideline 4*
Hold Your Relationship Sacred

YOU HONOR YOUR RELATIONSHIP by considering its sacredness. You should not allow the interference of others in it. You can keep its function special and singular; you can preserve the rituals practiced in and around it; you can protect it from outside influences that might taint it. The Us of your holy relationship belongs in a special place.

What therefore God hath joined together, let not man put asunder.

MARK 10:9 *KJV*

You Can Mend Your Relationship

Since you both "own" your holy relationship, each partner holds a responsibility to fix it. You may need some outside guidance, but no one can do it for you. Communicate with each other, persevere in your search for help, and be patient with the mending process. Don't expect someone else to miraculously fix your relationship for you. The holy work of reconciliation falls on each partner. You have come together to let the Holy Spirit work through you. Ask for the help of the Holy Spirit.

Guard the good treasure entrusted to you, with the help of the Holy Spirit living in us.

2 TIMOTHY 1:14 NRSV

25

Love Consciously – Live in the Moment

Remember to "love consciously" and you can enrich your relationship. It takes a conscious awareness, "living in the moment," to be intimate. Most of us are plagued by ghosts from our past that emerge when we find ourselves suddenly overexploiting, or overreacting to an issue. Later, we realize this issue reminds us of a particularly traumatic one in the past. Old ghosts can haunt this precious moment!

If anyone is in Christ, he is a new creation; the old has gone, the new has come!
2 CORINTHIANS 5:17 NIV

❧ *Guideline 5*

Forgiveness Is Essential in Your Relationship

ANOTHER GUIDELINE in a holy relation-ship is "Forgiveness is essential in your relationship." Forgiveness involves loving actions that restrain the impulse to attack. Gaining this forgiving perspective is not an inci-dental happening. It is not a simple switch in attitude; rather, it is a profound spiritual experi-ence occurring within the depth of our being. A sense of true forgiveness happens through this transformation within. It is essential to a holy relationship.

Bear with each other and forgive whatever griev-ances you may have against one another. Forgive as the Lord forgave you.

COLOSSIANS 3:13 NIV

Forgive Yourself First

It is essential to forgive yourself because God has already forgiven you. Christ tells us we are forgiven. Now you can extend that forgiveness to others. If you can look beyond your own fault and your own guilt, recognize your wrongs, and work fearlessly to correct them, you can grant others the freedom to heal, and to start anew just as you have done.

༄

Above all, love each other deeply, because love covers over a multitude of sins.

1 PETER 4:8 NIV

Forgiveness Is a Spiritual Happening!

To strive to forgive, to pretend to forgive won't work. Forgiveness must come from within the center of the spiritual self, from the knowledge that God is a forgiving God whose children abide in Divine Love. You are God's child and you are forgiven. Seeing yourself in this light will help you see your partner in the same light of forgiveness.

~

And be kind to one another, tenderhearted, for-giving one another, just as God in Christ also forgave you.

EPHESIANS 4:32 NKJV

Forgiveness Is a Gift to You

When you see forgiveness as an essential function in a relationship, you will find yourself released from the turmoil that originally beset you. You will experience peace once more. Ultimately, forgiveness becomes a gift to you. It is a decision to enter a process of healing; it is a decision to let go of anger and resentment, and to be at peace. With true forgiveness comes peace.

Let the peace of heart which comes from Christ be always present in your hearts and lives.
                                    COLOSSIANS 3:15 TLB

Learn from Forgiveness

Forgiveness does not imply that you submit to further wrongs, that you have to forget this incident, or that you fail to learn from this situation. Forgiveness does imply that you see the light of the spirit within the soul of your lover once again.

～

Live in harmony with one another.
ROMANS *12:16 NIV*

Let Go of Resentment and Anger

*F*ORGIVENESS IS THE KEY to a happy ending in any confrontation because it opens up a new chapter in the holy relationship. It reestablishes your ability to love by letting go of the resentment and anger. When you cherish resentment and anger, you allow your mind to be fed by fear; you become imprisoned by your own distortions. Love and fear cannot live in the same heart.

꒰

Be humble and gentle. Be patient with each other, making allowance for each other's faults because of your love.

EPHESIANS 4:2 TLB

Let Go of Guilt

UNLESS YOU SEE YOURSELF as forgiven by God, you may harbor guilt and constantly strive to make up for your imperfections. You could also judge and condemn others for their imperfections. Letting go of guilt means that you realize that you are innocent in the eyes of God. You release others from expectations, prejudices, and judgment. No one is guilty or not guilty in God's mind. You can live in love with your soul mate.

Live in love, as Christ loved us and gave himself up for us, a fragrant offering and sacrifice to God.
                              EPHESIANS 5:2 NRSV

❦ *Guideline 8*
Truth Is Essential

ANOTHER PRINCIPLE of sacredness in intimacy comes from understanding that "truth is essential." In a holy relationship, there are few barriers to expression. Because you can be honest with yourself, understanding your own truth, you can be honest with your loved one. Establish a childlike honesty about your feelings, values, needs, and dreams.

Therefore each of you must put off falsehood and speak truthfully... for we are all members of one body.

EPHESIANS 4:25 NIV

Be Honest!

When you operate a relationship on honest responses, the relating flows spontaneously. There is an issue to be solved, an answer to be found; the truth is expressed, the solution appears. There is no right or wrong: just an honest appraisal of the truth. If something distracts the relationship, if it is unacceptable to either of you, these things need to be looked at honestly.

In every sacred relationship, there is You, Me, and Us. If both lovers are truthful in their expressions, the relationship—the Us—will be honest and open as well. Loving expressions flow freely through the fabric of the relationship, making it strong in its honesty.

༄

Let everything you do reflect your love of the truth.

TITUS 2:7 TLB

Be Honest about Your Fears

You can be afraid, but that does not mean that your fears are grounded in reality. If you don't bring your fears out into the open, they will grow and, ultimately, immobilize you. You will start to make decisions out of fear, not love, and the relationship will suffer, or at best stagnate. Be honest about your fears.

But Jesus came and touched them and said, "Arise, and do not be afraid."
                                        MATTHEW 17:7 NKJV

Trust First, Test Later

*L*IKE CHILDREN, you need to "trust first" and to "test later." It is insulting and it is impractical to distrust a lover just because a previous one has let you down. Sometimes old hurts are carried into new relationships and we send negative messages to the wrong person. How much better it would be to trust unconditionally until it is proven unwise to offer that trust any longer.

❦

Trust in the Lord with all your heart, and lean not on your own understanding; in all your ways acknowledge Him, and He shall direct your paths.
                              PROVERBS 3:5, 6 NKJV

❧ *Guideline 10*
Live without Expectations

*E*ACH DAY there is something to celebrate if you accept life as it is, not as you might want it to be. Celebrate each day with your partner by accepting things as they are. Expectations of anything in life rob you of the present moment and cheat you of acceptance and peace. Goals are essential but expectations are "joy killers." Living without expectations allows each day to present itself as a wonderful gift to you and your love.

Therefore do not be anxious about tomorrow, for tomorrow will be anxious for itself. Let the day's own trouble be sufficient for the day.
                              MATTHEW 6:34 NRSV

Eliminate Pressure and Demands

Ironically, without expectations there is more coordination of goals. Simply by not forcing your will on your partner, they may come to the place where you are. That is not always the case, but pressure and demands often deny them the freedom to choose that direction. In addition, you are free in your choices when your partner never puts pressure on you to be anything but yourself. Love flows smoothly when there is no pressure, no expectations, no hidden demands.

Learn to put aside your own desires so that you will become patient and godly, gladly letting God have his way with you.

2 PETER 1:6 TLB

❧ *Guideline 11*
Detach with Love

*A*GOOD GUIDELINE in any relationship is to "detach with love." Detaching in a loving way simply means giving up the caretaking role and allowing loved ones to take responsibility for their own lives. Every time we assume responsibility for someone else's life we cripple them. Our greatest gift comes when we say, "I love you, so I am letting you go to experience this." When we give up controlling ways, we allow the space necessary for spiritual growth.

❧

Be an example to them of good deeds of every kind. Let everything you do reflect your love of the truth.

TITUS 2:7 TLB

Deal with Your Anger

A NGER IS A HEALTHY EMOTION—one that can prompt you into action, or alert you to problems within. It is therapeutic; it is necessary! Untamed anger, however, can destroy relationships. Ultimately, if you wish to live in peace, you have to understand how to deal with your anger. You need to own your anger. It comes from within you.

◦৲৴

Everyone should be quick to listen, slow to speak and slow to become angry.

JAMES 1:19 NIV

Deal with Anger Quickly

Problems arise when anger is not claimed and hangs around for days, months, or years. There is no intimacy in this situation. Do you give yourself permission to act out your anger? All relationships will be subject to an occasional quick expression of anger with a quick apology. Then comes the search within you for clues to the anger. Allowing constant outburst after outburst of damaging, unclaimed anger will erode the relationship. You need to own your anger and deal with it immediately.

"In your anger do not sin": Do not let the sun go down while you are still angry.

EPHESIANS 4:26 NIV

Find Out Where Your Anger Comes From

Finding out where your anger comes from is essential to living a spiritual life. You don't want to hurt others with angry, irrational responses. You don't really want to be out of control. Usually it takes an introspective self-questioning to get to the roots of your anger. It could be previously experienced neglect of parents, cruelty of siblings, or some injustice you had been forced to live with that triggers this anger. This is a very important issue, so set aside the time for this kind of introspection.

⸙

But the fruit of the spirit is... self-control.
GALATIANS 5:22, 23 NKJV

Feel Your Feelings

A LLOWING YOURSELF to "feel your feelings" is important. Instead of suppressing them or transferring them you need to face them. By facing your feelings, you resist the temptation of being overpowered by them. The objective is not eliminating anger or sadness but understanding these feelings and finding a healthy way to express them.

꒰

Do not quench the Spirit.
> 1 T HESSALONIANS 5:19 NKJV

Develop Emotional Maturity

Developing emotional maturity, striving for balance, and learning about your feelings are important, for you and your relationship. Unless both partners are able to handle anger, sadness, or fear, the whole relationship can become dysfunctional. When you become immobilized with emotions, or uncommunicative to those around you, your feelings may adversely affect your relationship.

❧

You know when I sit and when I rise; you perceive my thoughts from afar.

PSALM 139:2 NIV

Let Your Lover Own Their Own Feelings

One of the most destructive intrusions comes when you tell someone how they feel. Their emotions are their property so you don't need to evaluate or interpret them. This kind of boundary intrusion may cause resentment, and may make your partner feel invalidated. Let others define and explain their feelings; let them own them. Always ask them to explain what they feel.

꒰

Love is kind.

1 Corinthians 13:4 NIV

Know Your Needs and Express Them

A NOTHER GUIDELINE for holy relating is "Learn to know what you want and how to express that need." As you grow spiritually, you will change. Do not expect those around you to always fully understand how you are growing. Be clear! Tell them! Explain your new needs and concerns as they occur.

༄

Stay close to anything that makes you want to do right.

2 TIMOTHY 2:22 TLB

❦ *Guideline 15*

Peace Is Your Most Important Goal

WHENEVER YOU BECOME competitive with a loved one, you are destroying the unity of the holy relationship. In the spiritual sense, peace is your most important goal. Harmony is the key to right relating. Your goal should never be to get ahead, or to get back. That is not love, but aggression—war!

❧

Blessed are the peacemakers, for they shall be called sons of God.

MATTHEW 5:9 NKJV

Practices of
Holy Relationships

❧ *Practice 1*
Handling Confrontations

SOMETIMES THE DIFFERENCE between a fight and a confrontation is simply a matter of maintaining a loving, caring attitude. Powerful confrontations can be gentle when done with a show of concern for the other person. Immediate attention to any problem keeps it simple and right-sized. You might not want to be first to bring up a delicate issue; however, waiting only complicates the issue. Waiting causes a second issue... the issue of why you waited.

꒰ꕤ꒱

But the fruit of the Spirit is... gentleness.
                              GALATIANS 5:22, 23 NIV

When Do You Confront?

If a problem can't be taken care of immediately, it is always better to pick a time to talk when you can both be emotionally and spiritually present. Additionally, it is always better to pick a place where there will be no interruptions. When you confront, you can't expect 100 percent acquiescence to your every wish. Let your loved one save face in whatever way possible. Then, show appreciation for their cooperation.

She opens her mouth with wisdom, and the teaching of kindness is on her tongue.
                              PROVERBS 31:26 NRSV

Do I Understand the Issue?

Why is it that you argue, or agitate over things that seem inconsequential? Usually it is because that issue is not the real issue. So, when you get into something that seems a bit too testy, perhaps it is time to let it go. Later, with a little thought, you might better understand the real issue. You have a right to say, "I just don't know at this time."

Teach them the difference between what is holy and what is ordinary, what is pure and what is impure.

LEVITICUS 10:10 TLB

You Do Not Always Have to Agree

You do not always have to fight back to prove you are right or to exact an agreement from your partner. Sometimes it is appropriate to take a defenseless position. The judicious use of a defenseless position comes out of the belief that you are strong enough on your own, as God's child, to step back and retain your own sacred identity. If your partner does not agree with you, you do not lose anything, you remain the same—a perfect child of God. Leave them to their beliefs. Don't agree just to please your lover or you will feel untrue to your own spirit— cheated by yourself. Self-respect starts with you.

Do not conform any longer to the pattern of this world, but be transformed by the renewing of your mind.

ROMANS 12:2 NIV

Maintain a Spiritual Presence

A STRONG SPIRITUAL presence may disarm others, stop arguments before they start, and solve relational problems. It shows your partner that you are strong enough within yourself to avoid manipulation, accusations, guilt, resentment, and anger. Be vigilant about your part in all relating. Take your own inventory and focus on yourself first.

ॐ

Love is patient; love is kind.... It does not insist on its own way.

1 CORINTHIANS 13:4, 5 NRSV

Keep Your Own Autonomy

I N ORDER TO KEEP your own identity and
to develop your own gifts, it is essential to
keep your autonomy. Do the things you need
to do to grow spiritually. Don't expect your
partner to satisfy all of your needs. Know when
to reach deep down inside to your own insights
and knowledge. Your partner fell in love with the
You they first met, and that is the You that you
need to retain.

*Love each other... and take delight in honoring
each other.*

ROMANS 12:10 TLB

Dependent or Independent?

The challenge to a sacred relationship lies in determining when to be dependent and when to be independent. And what a challenge it is! There is a time to totally rely on the help of a loved one, and a time when it is inappropriate. Having the wisdom to "know when" is the spiritual work of your relationship.

༰

Remember in God's plan men and women need each other.

1 CORINTHIANS 11:11 TLB

Maintain a Balance

*I*T IS EASY to get caught up in doing everything "perfectly" and find yourself running out of "self." You need to understand that you can't be all things to all people, do everything perfectly, or give yourself entirely to another. There must be a balance in giving. Don't give your spirit away totally, or deplete your partner's spirit by "too much of a good thing." If a relationship is positive, it is hard not to want more of this good thing, but balance is the key.

ꝫ

Test all things; hold fast what is good.
                    1 *THESSALONIANS 5:21 NKJV*

❧ Practice 5
Negotiate Your Issues

I N NEGOTIATING an issue, your partner may be willing to give up too much and set himself or herself up for disaster in the future. Don't let that happen just to say you won points in the conflict. See their side! If your partner meets with disaster in the future, so do you. Refuse to accept a concession from your partner that will be destructive to them, or one to which you know they are unable to commit. Negotiate to a comfortable place for your partner—one that is equally comfortable for you.

The wisdom that comes from heaven is first of all pure; then peace-loving, considerate, submissive, full of mercy and good fruit, impartial and sincere.

JAMES 3:17 NIV

Ask: How Important Is It?

How important is the issue to you? That is the question! There are issues that are so important that you must stand firm on those issues. If you have a history as a fair, compromising person, then you will probably be heard by your partner when you need to stand firmly. By compromising on smaller issues, you can assure your future negotiating position in your relationship.

‿

Though I speak with the tongues of men and of angels, and have not charity, I am become as sounding brass, or a tinkling cymbal.
1 CORINTHIANS 13:1 KJV

Stand Firm When Needed

GIVING IN TO KEEP conflict away does not demonstrate strength. It suggests weakness and a general lack of courage on the part of the partner making all the concessions. The partner who is winning all the time develops an unrealistic perception of being right all the time. That kind of unbalance erodes the relationship.

Stand firm. Let nothing move you. Always give yourselves fully to the work of the Lord.
1 CORINTHIANS 15:58 NIV

Compromise When Needed

THE KEY TO NEGOTIATION is win/win. Basically it works this way. Don't try to be one up, or you will lose. You merely set up another negative situation that invites another confrontation. Negotiation should leave part of the relationship intact. It means giving up some things that are not asked for when you see that concession is a more productive course for the overall relationship.

༕

Remember the words of the Lord Jesus, that He said, "It is more blessed to give than to receive."
ACTS 20:35 NKJV

❦ *Practice 8*
Be Silent When Needed

S ILENCE! One kind is holy and purposeful. It is the kind that gives space, some time to think and become spiritually nourished. It is a simple request for distance to obtain perspective, to meditate, to go inside of self. This is holy silence.

A time to tear, and a time to sew; a time to keep silence, and a time to speak.

ECCLESIASTES 3:7 NKJV

Avoid Punitive Silence

Living as a child of God does not include behaviors like punitive silence. Powerful emotions may drive you to run and hide, to isolate, to avoid. Don't! It isn't worth it. The damage you do to your relationship will far outweigh the relief you get.

After taking a few moments to collect your thoughts, try to stay in a loving place with the issues at hand. Unholy silence screams out, "I won't talk to you because I am angry and I want to punish you." Unholy silence is a form of emotional abuse.

Be an example to them of good deeds of every kind.

TITUS 2:7 TLB

Don't Sulk in the Corner

Sulking in the corner is for children. In a holy relationship, you don't need to employ silence as a kind of violence against one another. There is no need to feel so degraded that you can't communicate. At the base of every discussion is the realization that both lovers are holy, perfect—children of God.

See that no one renders evil for evil to anyone, but always pursue what is good both for yourselves and for all.

1 Thessalonians 5:15 NKJV

❧ *Practice 9*
Apologize

ALWAYS TAKE TIME to look at your part in the problem. What can you own? Were you too abrupt? Uncompromising? Insensitive? Now is the time to admit to your part in this. However, apologize only for the things in your behavior that you know you did wrong. Apologize—and then, in the future, correct them. Your change in behavior may help your partner with his or her anger.

~

Be completely humble and gentle; be patient, bearing with one another in love.

EPHESIANS 4:2 NIV

Listen

*L*ET YOUR LOVER know you hear them. It is crucial that you feed back to them what they are saying. This feedback breaks down barriers in communication. Really listen and really see the person. Interpret their eyes, their body movements. Tell them you understand what they are saying to you.

ᘒ

Let me see your countenance, let me hear your voice; for your voice is sweet, and your countenance is lovely.

SONG OF SOLOMON 2:14 NKJV

Take Time and Space

TAKE THE TIME and space to think an issue through, to clarify your part in it. Then make a decision about how it can be handled. With this clarity of mind, go back to your partner and address the problem. When there is any doubt about your motives, or your emotional input into the situation, you may need to take another objective look at the situation from the distance of some elapsed time. "Time-outs" are not defeats. They aid negotiations.

‿კ⁊

Whatever is true, whatever is noble, whatever is right, whatever is pure, whatever is lovely, whatever is admirable—if anything is excellent or praiseworthy—think about such things.
                               PHILIPPIANS 4:8 NIV

❦ *Practice 12*
Reflection

REFLECTION! It doesn't cost money, can't be seen or felt, but it is essential to your spirit. It is through reflection and meditation that you escape the things of the world and open yourself to the spiritual. Understand your need for reflection. Be contemplative—think about your life, your relationship, the world around you, and your place in that world.

༄

Now we have received, not the spirit of the world, but the Spirit who is from God, that we might know the things that have been freely given to us by God.

1 CORINTHIANS 2:12 NKJV

Feed Your Soul

The healing of aloneness is powerful! It connects you to God, bringing you back to your relationship with a recharged spirituality. Have you hungered for solitude, without even knowing that you needed it until you were alone? Feed your soul!

⁂

And when you draw close to God, God will draw close to you. Let your hearts be filled with God alone to make them pure and true to him.
                                        JAMES 4:8 TLB

❦ *Practice 13*
Ask God for Help

EACH DAY IT IS WISE to begin the day by asking God to help guide your primary relationship, and each night give thanks for that guidance. Ask the Holy Spirit to flow between you and guide you in all interactions. Prayer reaps benefits for you and your lover.

∽

Pray in the Spirit on all occasions with all kinds of prayers and requests.

EPHESIANS 6:18 NIV

❦ *Practice 14*

Prayer

BUILD A STRONG relational bond in the ritual of common prayer. It can be just once in awhile, or a daily occurrence. There is something in admitting to each other that you seek a higher power to help your relationship. It sets priorities straight and validates the relationship as a holy relationship.

᠅

Love the Lord and follow his plan for your lives.
Cling to him and serve him enthusiastically.
JOSHUA 22:5 TLB

Honor Special Moments

Special moments deserve prayer. Prayer can be for general guidance for the two of you, for special graces to endure a situation, for acceptance, or simply to praise or thank God. Prayer can be shared meditative readings. Why not add this practice to your relationship?

Therefore I tell you, whatever you ask for in prayer, believe that you have received it, and it will be yours.

MARK 11:24 NIV

Touch

MANY TIMES LOVERS get so involved in everyday activities they forget about their need to be touched. Therefore, they lose its therapeutic value. Even with a good relationship, there can be periods of touch deprivation. Slow down—get away and get in touch with each other. Touching brings your relationship back into focus!

৵৲

Arise, come, my darling; my beautiful one, come with me.

SONG OF SOLOMON 2:13 NIV

Nonsexual Touch

Nonsexual touch can be especially meaningful because it implies a kind of caring for the total person—one that goes beyond physical attraction. Your touch can be as simple as a supportive hand on the shoulder when there is some difficulty, or as extensive as a back rub or massage. Touching says you affirm your love. It says you approve of your lover, of their body. It makes the relationship real. Touch is important.

Be kindly affectionate to one another with brotherly love, in honor-giving preference to one another.

ROMANS 12:10 NKJV

Sensual Touching

Sensual touching provides a prelude for a sexual encounter, but it also provides affirmation: a silent support, a credibility for the whole relationship. Touching is just another part of knowing each other, another silent love message to your lover.

How delightful is your love…. How much more pleasing is your love…
                    SONG OF SOLOMON 4:10 NIV

❦ *Practice 16*
Be Sexual

S EXUAL UNION with a beloved becomes a sacred act of joining not only of the bodies but of the souls as well. Sexual energy becomes spiritual energy when you totally trust yourself and your partner with your body, and with your spirit as well. In a holy relationship you have a permanent sexual bond that ties you together in the oneness of each other. It is not an attraction to the body, or to sizes and shapes of body parts, but a love of the whole person. Physical sexuality alone can be aggressively lustful. Spiritual sexuality is sheer bliss.

༼

The two will become one flesh. So they are no longer two, but one.

MARK 10:8 NIV

Take Care of Sexual Needs

You need to be conscious of both your own and your partner's sexual needs, blending these desires into a satisfying sexual life. Find out about your partner's sexual habits, their sex drive. Be free to make this very important subject an area for open discussion. It is too important to be overlooked. Any good sexual relationship is marked by certain ritualistic touches, signals that become the language of sexuality. It can include places, times, fragrances, and candlelight. Sexual rituals enrich the depth of sexual contact.

⌇

Kiss me again and again, for your love is sweeter than wine.

SONG OF SOLOMON *1:2 TLB*

Have Fun

Your lover has a child within them, just as you do. Finding a way to communicate with that child will open up your relationship to more intimacy. Allow your partner to approach your child as well. You do not have to be an adult all the time. Be a little crazy, irresponsible, and fun-loving once in awhile. You can laugh uncontrollably at times, tease playfully, run and hide and seek. Maybe it will be a pillow fight, or a playful wrestling match, or sledding or ice skating—that's OK. Have fun together!

He will fill your mouth with laughter and your lips with shouts of joy.

JOB 8:21 NIV

❦ *Practice 17*

Affirm Your Love

*A*FFIRM YOUR LOVED ONE! Seize the moment and speak those positive messages. How often do you think something loving but fail to say it? When you speak loving words, you add to your holy relationship. When you hear a positive message in your mind, stop and say it! Nurture your lover, not in a solicitous way, but in an honest way. Always look to the good in your lover; speak of it; be a positive partner, and have a positive relationship. Communication is not just about conversing with another: it is about pulling those positive thoughts out into the open and letting your partner know that you appreciate them.

Pleasant words are like honeycomb, sweetness to the soul and health to the bones.
PROVERBS 16:24 NKJV

Give Special Gifts

Pay attention to the special things your partner likes. Surprise them now and then. Gifts don't have to be expensive, because it really is the thought that counts. Write a note, make a card, or cook a special meal. Unexpected loving gestures are appreciated. Call just to say something loving. Write a nice letter. There are so many ways to show appreciation—be creative!

꒰꒱

And God is able to make all grace abound toward you, that you, always having all sufficiency in all things, have an abundance for every good work.

2 CORINTHIANS 9:8 NKJV

Be Patient

*I*N A HOLY RELATIONSHIP, there are no reprisals for weak moments. We all need to be able to admit that we are in a "bad space," filled with grief, or disappointed, or even acting like a child. Helping your partner to get through these difficult moments is the work of sacred relating. The crisis can be as serious as the death of a parent, or as simple as a dent in a new car. Give your lover time, space, gentle handling, and gentle listening. Help is not always about doing! Just understand and be patient.

May God who gives patience, steadiness, and encouragement help you to live in complete harmony with each other—each with the attitude of Christ toward the other.

ROMANS 15:5 TLB

Watch Your Words

W ATCH YOUR LANGUAGE! Words like "you should," "you must," or "ought to" always indicate an attempt to control. Everyone needs to come to their own place of discovery without being told what to do. If your partner doesn't come to their own decisions, they won't truly own those decisions, and resentment will build when they feel forced to carry those decisions to completion.

෭

Set a guard, O Lord, over my mouth; keep watch over the door of my lips.

PSALM 141:3 NKJV

Develop Rituals

RITUALS BY THEIR very nature mark and move the natural process of life. A relationship that develops an intimate sacredness through rituals has depth, tradition, and structure. When you go for breakfast every Saturday morning, you are building a ritual. These acts become sacred. Together, you can build images and memories to share. You can find special sanctuaries where you can connect tradition to your relational life. Love is built every day. Love is an active participation in life—a tapestry of love rituals!

Love each other... and take delight in honoring each other.

ROMANS 12:10 TLB

Purposes of
Holy Relationships

To Teach Love

WHAT LESSON does your relationship teach? Are you dedicated to a higher purpose or committed to being right all the time, having your ego fed, and all of your needs met? You will teach as you live; you will teach as you relate. That is certain! What statement does your relationship make?

Let us love one another, for love comes from God. Everyone who loves has been born of God and knows God. Whoever does not love does not know God, because God is love.

1 JOHN 4:7, 8 NIV

To Communicate with God

*T*EACH ONLY LOVE, for that is what you are. Use affirmations everyday to bring you back to God. Ask that you be willing to teach only love. Love enters by invitation. Ask God for help. Say to God, "I give you my part in this relationship. Heal me with your Love."

The closer you are to your spiritual center, the more love you will bring to your relationship. Say, "God is the love in which I live." "God is the strength in which I trust." Keep God close to you, and teach only love.

Be still, and know that I am God.

PSALM 46:10 NIV

To Communicate with Others

*I*N EACH HOLY relationship is the ability to communicate instead of separate. The instant a thought of separation comes to mind, ask Divine Love to take it and replace it with a loving thought. Release sadness and anger, and your judgments and criticisms of others, and of yourself. A holy relationship is a common state of mind, where both partners give errors gladly to correction, that both may happily be healed as one.

༅

And this I pray, that your love may abound still more and more in knowledge and all discernment.

PHILIPPIANS 1:9 NKJV

❦ *Purpose 4*
To Heal

I T IS IN A holy relationship that we fulfill the divine plan for healing of the world. Our love heals us and others. Let the expression of love in your relationship uplift and inspire you and others.

ↄ

Now glory be to God who by his mighty power at work within us is able to do far more than we would ever dare to ask or even dream of— infinitely beyond our highest prayers, desires, thoughts, or hopes.

EPHESIANS 3:20 TLB

To Give Your Relationship to God

GIVE YOUR RELATIONSHIP to Divine Love to be used for a higher purpose. Your togetherness is sacred. You are sacred— both of you! Together you can become teachers of God just by exchanging the holy energy of love. Let your love teach others by its presence.

Allow Divine Love to lift you from all that would hurt you or your partner. Ask God to give you all the tools needed to continue to be blessed in wholeness and unity.

Whether you turn to the right or to the left, your ears will hear a voice behind you, saying, "This is the way; walk in it."

ISAIAH 30:21 NIV

❦ Purpose 6
To Practice Courage

WHENEVER YOU HAVE difficulty, ask yourself if you have given your power to the negative situation. When we focus on what we perceive as lacking in our relationship, that seeming lack grows and becomes all we see. Do you want to see your loved one as guilty, or innocent? How would Christ view you? If you judge others, you judge yourself. Once you take charge of cleaning up your own negative thinking patterns and beliefs, you can proceed with courage.

But those who hope in the Lord will renew their strength. They will soar on wings like eagles; they will run and not grow weary, they will walk and not be faint.

ISAIAH 40:31 NIV

To Have Faith

ALWAYS HOLD WITHIN your heart the conviction of a holy relationship, knowing that love can be profound and easy, without conflict and struggle. Call on the Holy Spirit, asking that your faith be magnified until it is powerful enough to see you and your loved one through any difficulty.

The Lord is good, a refuge in times of trouble. He cares for those who trust in him.

NAHUM 1:7 NIV

Stand Together in Light

God loves you both, equally as one. He lets his light shine through you to each other. You are not joined together in the ways of the world, but in this spiritual light of God's love, which is so holy and so perfect that nothing can darken the place where you stand together.

✑

I have come into the world as a light, so that no one who believes in me should stay in darkness.
                                            JOHN 12:46 NIV

❦ *Purpose 8*

To Experience Joy

REMEMBER THAT "God's Will for you is Joy." That means you can expect to be happy in your relationship. All you have to do is call upon the presence of Divine Love to be available to you and your lover. It isn't God's will that we need to fear but our own. No one can find joy while attempting to change another or blame another. We accept who we are, we accept who our lover is—a child of God. We accept God as our primary relationship. Then, step aside and let God's will be done.

I have told you this so that my joy may be in you and that your joy may be complete.

JOHN 15:11 NIV

❦ *Purpose 9*

To Know Peace through the Acceptance of God's Will

A CCEPTANCE BRINGS joy and peace. When we can't accept life's difficulties and refuse to understand that in *all* things there is some good, some lesson to learn, we are not doing the will of God. God's ultimate plan is that we live with joy in our heart. Our acceptance of life brings peace.

You are not in charge of your relationship. God is! You are only in charge of yourself and how you relate to God. By turning your life and will over to God, you will find peace!

Peace I leave with you; my peace I give you. I do not give to you as the world gives. Do not let your hearts be troubled and do not be afraid.

JOHN 14:27 NIV

❦ *Purpose 10*

To Remove All Barriers to Love

YOUR TASK IS NOT to seek for love, but merely to seek and find all of the barriers within yourself that you have built against it. A holy relationship is a sacred union that has removed the barriers to love.

It takes a strong commitment to your own sacredness to maintain such a relationship; yet, paradoxically, once you reach this spiritual plateau, an intrinsic peace and joy develops within you. Naturally, you attract what you emanate and join with another who has also found love within. It is this loveliness that others notice. It is this peace and joy that make it work. It is there for anyone if they but ask for it!

And now abide faith, hope, love, these three; but the greatest of these is love.

1 CORINTHIANS 13:13 NKJV